Indian Summer

Howard J. Kogan

In Dahra Heyn

Best wishes,

Howard J. Kogan

SQUARE CIRCLE PRESS
VOORHEESVILLE, NEW YORK

Indian Summer

Published by
Square Circle Press LLC
137 Ketcham Road
Voorheesville, NY 12186
www.squarecirclepress.com

Printed in the United States of America on acid-free, durable paper.
ISBN-13: 9780983389743
ISBN-10: 0983389748
Library of Congress Control Number: 2011933354

Publisher's Acknowledgments
Cover design by Richard Vang, Square Circle Press. Cover image photograph by Libby Kogan.

"Photograph," "Bailey at the Museum" and "Zamboni" were also published in *Award-Winning Poems from the Smith's Tavern Poet Laureate Contest, 2010 Edition* (Square Circle Press). "Three Jokes for Science," "Evolution" and "Winter Wren" were also published in *Award-Winning Poems from the Smith's Tavern Poet Laureate Contest, 2011 Edition* (Square Circle Press).

The author's acknowledgments appear elsewhere in this book.

To purchase additional copies of this book, please visit bookstores in the Albany, New York area, or visit us online at *www.squarecirclepress.com*.

Contents

This book is for the people who live in my poems

and the people who read and listen to them.

I am grateful for your companionship.

My world would be very lonely without you.

I don't know who wrote these poems,

I found them in my mind and wrote them

down to bewitch, seduce and entertain you.

I did it to keep you close.

Acknowledgments

I am deeply appreciative of all the members of my family, friends, and fellow poets who have encouraged and valued my work. Muses come in many forms and I need and love you all.

Indian Summer

Indian Summer

When I imagine my life as a year,
the autumnal equinox has long passed.
Dry crackling leaves darken to mold,
the air chills, the darkness lingers
at dawn and hurries the dusk.
A silver frost is over all.

Then, as if Remorse was a weather god,
the summer returns, sweet tranquil days,
follow in a row like farm stand pumpkins.
The harvest moon lights the cleared field,
casting the idled reaper as looming apparition.

Then, too soon, a day arrives and without lament,
the clear weather high flees with the North wind,
the snow descends and stillness is over all.
After the solstice the light begins its slow return —
and the analogy fails.

Bailey at the Museum

We are at the Williams College Museum of Art —
the exhibition of Gerald Murphy's seven paintings,
plus a collection of memorabilia which announces
Gerald and Sara Murphy are — the celebrated Murphy's —
friends of F. Scott Fitzgerald, Hemingway and Porter.

Bailey at six breezes past the paintings as if on roller skates.
She enters the next gallery and announces, "This is Egyptian!"
and has to be summoned back to look at the hieroglyphics.
She has seen them before and when I try to explain how old
these panels are, it is beyond boring. At sixty-seven I am

the oldest element in her universe and even my age is beyond
her imagining. When I tell her with my sixty-seven and her six we
could make two thirty-six year olds — her brow knits — briefly.
She slows to look at a series of nudes, and smiling conspiratorially
stage whispers to her mother, my daughter, they are "Inappropriate

for someone my age." I wander off to look at the Murphy
memorabilia and discover the tragedy of both young son's early
death from tuberculosis and meningitis.
There are drawings the children made and I am looking
at them when Bailey finds me. These drawings, so like her own,

4

slow her pace. A brown horse, a white sailboat, neatly rendered
in familiar crayon colors. I do not tell her the Murphy's sons
are dead. Hemingway, Fitzgerald, the Murphy's, the Porter's,
the Egyptians, probably every painter of every work
she has skated past today, is dead. I joked once about dying

and she cried. She has an idea I can wait for her and we will
marry. She is my future but I will not be hers. A few more spins
around the museum and she will round the corner a young woman,
do her thumbs up salute and skate out of our lives into her own.
And we will be her past, staring, mouths agape, full of wonder

and loss.

Nikolas

Born after a pregnancy punctuated
by dread, IV drips and calamity,
he was found "perfect" at birth.
Then there was a small problem,
probably "nothing to worry about."

Then it was beyond what could be managed
at the local hospital and he was transferred
to one with a Neo-Natal Intensive Care Unit.

Then he was dying and there was nothing to be done
but to pass him from mother's arms to father's arms
until what life there was, was over.

But it was not over for us.
We had waited too long to lose him now.
We refused, as is the right of the grieving.
Each mourner holding firm brought him home
as if being nowhere enabled him to be everywhere.

Dead these six years after a life measured in hours,

he is in the first grade now.

He plays soccer poorly like his father,

and bosses his little sisters around.

We glimpse him everywhere.

The shared secret we cannot share,

each imagining it is ours alone.

I close my eyes and see him;

tell him stories about my life,

a better life than the one I had.

We all see him,

but we don't talk about it.

Someone might say the wrong thing

and we would lose him again,

then where would we be?

A family of crazed porcelains,

each, a touch away from shattered.

Zamboni

I am lying in a hospital bed surrounded by the concerned.
I can remember being in the garden, when my head exploded.
I cannot move or speak. My living will comes to mind.

It is a Chinese menu of pain, misery and insult.
I had checked the no extra-ordinary measures from column A.
And the full pu-pu platter of pain medication from column B.

No one wants to suffer or be a burden or worse—a vegetable.
Yet now I feel oddly certain—things are going to be okay.
Did someone say, Vegetable?

They can be deceiving. Cauliflowers despite appearances
Are dopes. Broccoli is smarter. Broccoli rabe is a genius.
Beets have it over potatoes on most standardized tests.

Carrots are practically mute and can't really be tested.
When one of those New Age types talks about the wisdom
Of the carrot, let me tell you it's pure speculation.

Tomatoes and sweet corn are so narcissistic I don't even like
To mention them. And the greens—the envy of the greens—
Kale wants to be spinach—spinach wants to be lettuce—

Lettuce wants to be something sexy and Italian.
No, the ones I like, the ones I might aspire to, are
The alliums; an Ailsa Craig onion or perhaps a shallot …

Wait a minute—where is everyone going? Are they
Turning off the monitors? Pulling the plug?
I am drifting into twilight. I am surrounded by lights—flashing

Lights—they're everywhere. I am a Zamboni, one of a squadron
Of Zambonis snuffling across the ice, smoothing and polishing
the earth as if it were a jewel—something I hadn't noticed before.

Evolution

*"Homo sapiens are a tiny twig on an improbable branch of a
contingent limb on a fortunate tree." (Stephen Jay Gould)*

What Homo sapiens would believe such a thing?

In our heart of hearts we know
the first blue-green bacterium flipped
their little riboswitches and knitted
their strands of nucleotides dreaming of us.

Didn't the first paramecium point its microscopic
snout and twitch its cilia to hula over to us?
Just as the first amoeba stretched a shapely pseudopod
to tango in our direction?

In time they all found themselves in the Garden of Eden.
Looking up, as Adam and Eve looked down, admiring
their perfect reflection in the pond's mirrored surface.
It was at this moment on the spiral staircase of evolution

certainty begot doubt. The little strivers in the pond wondered

if perhaps they should've aimed at something less multi-cellular.

Wondered if it might still be possible to re-direct creation

toward sponges or perhaps fish.

Wondered if it might still be possible to snip

this twig before the awful weight of its self-

importance caused it to fall — carrying

the rest of creation with it.

Winter Wren

Received this morning, one winter wren,
a gift from Tux, our cat, who found it hopping
on the ground in the front garden like a vole,
which is what I thought it was,
and, to be frank, slowed my rescue.

When I called Tux, he left it,
but then, as though remembering
his manners, returned to fetch it in.
A last minute offering, the way you,
a person of good manners, might stop
at an all-night drugstore to pick up
a hostess gift after an impromptu
dinner invitation. Though none
was expected or needed.

So it was my fate to hold the tiny wren

through its final tremor and twitch,

its wiry legs pedaling slowly until it lay

loose headed in the manner of the dead.

Its chestnut feathers lifting at the

at the final moment, as if something

was released, and then subsiding

as the checker spotted breast stilled.

This poem is her epitaph.

Let the universe take note

of the loss of one young winter

wren, who died in my hand

while the ever hopeful Tux,

purred with pleasure,

and graciously waited,

for me to eat it.

Three Jokes for Science

When I was eight, an older boy
told me our town's two large
supermarkets; Stop and Shop and A & P
were merging to became Stop & P.
It was the high point of my first decade.
It still rates a smile in my seventh.
Which may be more evidence than I really wanted
that while youth is fleeting, immaturity is forever.

In my twenties there was the one
about the Englishman.
I confess I went through a phase
of loving everything English.
This may account for my affection,
for the Englishman who wore two monocles,
and made a spectacle of himself.

In my thirties there was the story
about this fellow who goes to Miami
for his annual vacation.
He sees a beautiful woman
in his hotel lobby and winks.
She whispers, "I'm selling."

He whispers, "I'm buying."
A few weeks later he's at the doctors'
and learns he has gonorrhea.
The next year, it's the same week,
the same hotel, the same woman.
She whispers, "I'm selling."
He whispers, "What are you selling this year —
kidney stones?"

You may be asking,
"How are three old jokes a poem?"
Don't ask. Actually I am conducting
a scientific experiment,
involving all the dead poets,
from Gilgamesh in the Twentieth Century BC
to Ginsberg in the Twentieth Century AD.

The experiment theorizes this poem
will cause forty centuries of dead poets
to spin in their graves with enough velocity
to spark a few new ideas.
The ideas we have now aren't working.

Petroglyph

I am at Salt Creek in Arches National Park staring
at a petroglyph pecked into the desert varnish on a red
sandstone bluff. I came here alone on a footpath marked
by cairns, but now a tour bus is arriving.

I've never been here before, yet as I stand here,
the whole petroglyph; the people on horseback,
the horned sheep, the coyotes, look familiar. The figures
on horseback are Ute's. The drawing's about one-hundred

and fifty years old, from a time when the first pioneers
were arriving. Today I know something the Ute's could not –
it's the beginning of their end. In a hundred and fifty years
the people looking at this drawing will have stepped out

of an air conditioned bus after flying half way across a world
the Ute's did not know existed. They will wear sun screen,
talk on cell phones and barely listen as a tour guide talks
about petroglyphs and points to this scene.

They are eager to get their photographs and move
on to lunch and margaritas. None of us is a native;
the Ute's are travelers from Asia over the Bering land bridge.
The horses and sheep were brought by Spanish missionaries.

We know this — anyone or anything that can move — will move.
As though life itself is restless, as though life itself is searching —
for what? — greener pastures? We will find them soon enough.
After our final migration, when we lie staring with unblinking

eyes at the green pastures overhead.
The tour returns to the bus. I stand a while longer
staring at the petroglyph; the sun peers over my shoulder
as we both ponder the scenes familiarity.

I feel like I am looking for something. Then suddenly
I see it down in the corner of the petroglyph. It's
a figure I hadn't noticed before, he's walking
up the trail I just followed, it must be me.

The Year We Got Older

We knew it the autumn before
or should have, it was that plain.
The exhaustion that fierce.

Grateful for the excuse of a hard frost,
the garden tools were left in the shed
clotted with earth and rust.

We walked away from that garden
the way people walk — stunned — from
a factory that's shuttered.

No tilling done, no rye seed sown,
no manure spread, no harvest pride,
no thought of return.

But winter rest and woodstove heat
fooled us into forgetting what we knew.
Friends sent seeds promising the best

tomato ever, squash the taste of roasted
chestnuts, homey soup beans passed
like genes from generation to generation.

It got so we could imagine another year
of working together and growing the garden.
They were the best times, scrutinizing catalogs,

meditating on seed orders, dream gardening.
It's the kind of enthusiasm that's possible
when your body doesn't have to pay the bill.

Spring came wet and late and winter dreaming
precipitated into work that needed doing.
We faced spring with more dread than hope,

me thinking only I was feeling that way,
she not wanting to spoil it for me. Each
hoping to keep their end up one more season.

Well we just about got it planted but what grew
grew without help from us. That was the end of it.
That was the last year we got older.

Community of Old Women

You will be joining the community of old women soon.
Making quilts for the Children's Hospital,
volunteering at the Community Tag Sale,
calling friends to check and chat.
Whatever chat can be found
in lives thinned by the rasp of age and loss.

The creak and groan of wind and house
will not rouse you; yet your sleeping hand
will slide across the sheet to find
the awakening chill of missing me.
The first snows of winter, welcomed once,
will bring only a drift of memories

witnessed by you and the silent moon.
The children, of course, will visit.
They're in there fifties now, how odd
we still do not have another word for them.
In truth, everyone is so busy these days,
most days, most days, you will be alone.

Not the welcome reprieve from too much,
but the unquiet quiet of loneliness.
You will be a sister among so many
sisters in the loss of their husbands
in the absence of close family,
in the absence of being needed.

Lives measured by ills, lacks and limits
focusing on now, on being careful.
You will be in the tribe of women left behind
when the men who had been their lives,
(though none would ever put it that way)
were lowered slowly, with curious care,

for a cargo of so little worth,
into the hold of a patient earth.
We were not men who thought about
heaven or hell or ever expected much.
But in the community of women,
women who had been left before when we

$\rightarrow$

went to war, when the idea of coming back

was no more certain than hope. They could

still recall the feeling of our being away.

Not that anyone thought it was the same

or would even think to speak of it,

yet somewhere tucked like a single sock

in the chest of drawers of forgotten memory

nested an idea of comfort and promise

for those left behind — the hint of a return.

Something to wait for, a reason to keep things nice.

Yes, and keep a good dress ready, something that would

do nicely to meet a returning ship or — to set off on your own.

Photograph

I am looking though my parent's photo album,

and see a photograph that I still remember.

We are standing in front of our house, the picture,

taken with my sister's boxy Brownie, is black

and white with scalloped edges.

We were going to visit my grandmother when

a neighbor, Mrs. Chapman, offered to take our picture.

My mother and father are standing together,

my sister — seven years older — is next to my mother,

and I am next to my father.

But there is a space between my father and myself.

And, as a result, the frame of the photo cuts off my left arm.

I liked that picture then and I am pleased to find it again;

it was the way we were.

The three of them and me, a little

off to the side, a little out of the picture.

The Isolation of Old Men

I like baked beans — always have — they're easy.

Eat 'em cold or put the can right on the burner.

No dirty dishes. Hot dogs too — they're easy

and eggs — anybody can make eggs.

Or I get take-out — I don't like to sit there,

one at a table for two — I take it home — eat with the TV.

I used to take walks most days but

after the dog died that year after Mary;

there didn't seem any point to taking a walk.

It just wasn't something I did anymore.

The kids worry about me,

they call and I appreciate that, I really do.

But I don't have much to say,

not much happens here anymore.

I like to hear about the little ones — I do.

They're far away; I don't see them much,

except holidays, we do holidays best we can.

I'm not complaining — I had my life — a good one.

When we were young and the kids were small,
even when they grew up — Mary and I —
we enjoyed our life.
Then I retired and Mary got so sick so soon,
we had plans but she never wanted to be
too far from the doctor.

Mary was quite a woman in her day,
but the sickness took everything out of her.
She was never really the same
after that first operation, never the same.
We did take the trip to the Cape,
salty air, lobsters, corn on the cob right on a pier.

We both said we had a good time there.
My daughter thinks I should get another dog,
but I am too old.
What if I died — and left the poor dog —
you know, all alone.
It's not right to do that to an animal.

The Great War

She was barely six in 1914 and still
learned enough in the next three years
to fuel a lifetime of bad days, worse nights.

In truth,
I never knew the truth.
She rarely spoke of it.
Her father came to the United States
a month before the war began,
the others were to come a month later.
The month lasted three years.

Her mother, a brother, a sister and
herself, the eldest girl, survived
the War attached to a burial detachment.
When the front moved, as it often did,
they would become attached
to the opposing army's burial detachment.
Her mother baked bread and cooked
for the soldiers, that much I was told.

The soldiers got drunk every night,
the Cossacks were worse than the Germans
because the Cossacks hated the Jews more
or because the Cossacks drank more.
They would bang on their door and
threaten to kill the Jews. Then what happened?
She never said. Use your imagination.

Soon enough I stopped asking questions.
Soon enough I understood she was the answer.

She was a one trick magician, a vanishing act.
She was always somewhere else, as if
listening to distant thunder.
"What are you thinking about?" I would ask.
"Nothing, I'm fine, just tired."
I'd say, "You can't think about nothing."
"I can think about nothing," was the reply.

Whatever she went through she survived.
But what remains are only the remains,
a reflection in the mirror, a flattened self.
War can do that to soldiers and to civilians too.   →

She lived in fear of the door not holding.
In the moment before the door gives way,
between the imagined horror
and the horror realized.
She lived in those memories,
staring at scenes she could never narrate
or she lived, eyes squeezed shut, in their wake.

What she saw killed her.
Not quite like the soldiers
but not so different either.
After the Great War her life was over and
living another sixty-six years didn't change a thing.

I have lived these years with this question,
how can I wake the dead without killing them?
She was my first patient, the person who taught me
to love Zombies and to mourn for them.
Please mother, can we bury the dead?
Can we say a prayer for them and for us?
And finally—at long last—live.

Heroic Companions

How we love the stories of dogs
dragging unconscious owners
out of burning buildings.

Of cats who dial 9-1-1 to save
a family overcome by gas.

Of the wise goldfish who wakes
the sleeping child by splashing her
as smoke creeps under the door.

How comforted we are by their heroics —
how desperate we are to be saved.

Dreaming of Leah

Fifty-eight years after her death
I dreamt of my grandmother Leah.

My father and I visited her on Sundays
the long, silent drive to Brooklyn,
a meditation on what could not be said.

When we arrive, she ignores my father,
prayerfully presses my hands between hers,
and smiles as one tear, then another,
rolls down her face. I stretch on tip toes
to kiss lips that pucker and quiver to meet mine
like carp rising in a dark pond.

A few minutes later my father dismisses me
to explore the foreign land outside her door.
I return, as told, an hour later
to eat a slice of oily halvah.
Leah pets my head and whispers —
"a brocheh ahf dein kop — mein Amerikanisher boychik."

Yiddish was the only language Leah spoke or understood.
The throaty sounds of the language intrigued me
but I cannot understand the words or even
separate one word from the next as they tumble out.
I wander the small apartment looking
at the Diego Rivera prints and browsing
through books in English she cannot read.
Her goodbye repeats her welcome in every sadness.

My grandfather Jonah was a teamster.
A Brooklyn cowboy, as I thought of it,
leading his horse and wagon through
people crowded streets lined by pushcarts.
Each day he tried to squeeze a living
moving equally poor evicted fellow immigrants
from the curb of one dilapidated building to another
offering an inducement of two months free rent.

A few months later, after the two free months
and the one paid in advance, he would move them again.
The horse was the business and a mouth to feed
and when money was short the horse ate first.
When it was very short only the horse ate.   →

31

Jonah died young and my father Sol

and his sister Minnie, the two eldest,

went to live at the Brooklyn Hebrew Orphan Asylum.

Leah cared for the three youngest.

There was always that split in the family,

Sol and Minnie and Joe, Jesse and Freda.

The sad, angry, barely schooled older children

and the City College attending, successful younger ones.

The ones she left at the orphanage visited her more.

Years later I visited her on her first day in a nursing home.

I can still see her in the corner of her room screaming

and spitting at anyone who went near her, even my father.

I was quickly pushed out of the room into a hallway lined

with old women tossed onto wheelchairs like soiled linens.

As I walked by they pulled their wheelchairs closer

shuffling feet dog paddling, their slippers hissing,

bent fingers reaching out to me, thick tongues

sliding in and out with the effort, leaving fangs

of spit swinging from hairy upturned chins.

Bulging wet eyes pin-balled from side to side

as their voices rose and fell, croaked and gurgled,

calling out to missing children in Yiddish.

I ran — heart pounding, until I reached the outer door,
my face throbbing — red with fear and shame.

Later I asked if grandma was okay.
My father said they had given her something,
something to make her sleep.
Bruce's dog had been given something,
something to make her sleep
and it killed her dead.
I did not know which sleep he meant and did not ask.

A few weeks later he was called to the nursing home.
He went alone now and it was dark when he returned.
I remember the moment he walked in the back door,
my mother had gotten up when she heard the car door.
She was standing in the middle of the kitchen.
He walked in and said to her, "it's all over."
They hugged, not something that happened often,
and I felt a chill, grew smaller and said nothing.

$\longrightarrow$

Over the years I knew Leah she had changed
but they were very different changes than I saw
in my mother's mother. She, another Leah,
softened with age and rounded.
But the older my father's mother got,
the more tautly her skin stretched between stiff bones,
the darker her complexion browned,
the more she looked like an Indian.

In the dream I am at an Indian encampment.
It is near Salt Creek in the Great Basin desert.
As the dream begins I am walking down a slight rise
toward a group of people gathered at a blazing bonfire.
The bonfire brightly illuminated the people
while casting dark shadows behind them.
Leah was standing near the fire
wearing a beaded buckskin dress.
I knew she was my grandmother, but also a tribal elder
tempered by the hardness of her life.
I saw my father a few yards away, my son and daughter
stood at his side, watching Leah and smiling broadly.
I was happy to see my father with them,
the grandchildren he had never met in life.

I turned to look at Leah and as I did

she pulled a piece of meat from the fire

and used her teeth to rip a strip off.

Her eyes searched the crowd,

I knew she was looking for me.

Our eyes met and her face filled

with that same smile and tears

as she held the strip of meat out to me.

My Indian grandmother, marooned in Brooklyn

with her cowboy Jonah, had found her rightful place

in the Great Basin Desert. Transformed into the person

she never and always was and I was with her again.

The sadness of Brooklyn faded and we laughed

as I walked to her. Her real American grandson

had returned and all that had been lost — restored.

The Way We Met

I started going to St Ignatius of Loyola Roman
Catholic Church with my friend Matt on Saturday
afternoons, when he had to go to Confession.
It was cool and quiet there with only a soft murmuring
in the background, like a stream in deep woods.

Any noise, like when I dropped the kneeling bench,
sounded like thunder echoing in a cave, but turned no heads.
Sometimes I'd go there alone to sit and watch the old women
light candles and pray. No one talked to me until that day when
Father Pat suddenly appeared saying he was Father Pat,

and, was I okay? I liked the way he talked. It was the way
our neighbors talked who had come from Ireland.
Matt had told me about nice priests and mean priests so I knew
Father Pat was okay. If it had been Father Tom I'd have run.
Father Pat could tell I was crying. I don't know why, it was nothing

unusual. I don't remember what else he said; then he looked up,
saw you, and said, "Kathleen, show this fellow where he can
wash up, would you?" You looked at me and said, "Come on,"
and we walked, you leading the way as you always have,
down the stairs to the basement and a door with "LAVATORY"

printed in gold letters. You pointed and I went in to discover
Lavatory was Catholic for bathroom. You were waiting
in the hallway when I came out, a skinny girl wearing
the St. Ignatius of Loyola dark blue uniform. You asked
if I was new here and I said no, I was Jewish.

You didn't have any breasts then, but later
I would call the one Iggy and the other Lola
because of the two words I read on your chest.
I was too shy to look you in the eye.

Visiting for Jehovah

I was working on the tractor when a car came up the driveway.

Two men got out of an old deep blue Buick, smiling and talking.

"Nothing runs like a Deere," says the one who looks like a hard life

on two legs. "This Deere's not running at all," I say.

"Do you know what Last Days means?"

"What about Armageddon?" says the other.

"May we talk to you about God's plan?"

"I'm kind of busy right now."

"It's a good day to cut the grass," says hard life.

"I have to get the tractor started first."

"We'll leave you these magazines,

they explain all about it."

They turn to go but I call after them.

"Either of you guys know anything about tractors?"

"Saturday we work for the Lord, we talk about

Last Days – not tractor problems."

He pauses, as though remembering his Sunday
School manners, blushes at the neck and says,
"We are both mighty sorry for your trouble,
isn't that right Bob?"

"Yes, and if we did know how to fix the tractor
we surely would, wouldn't we Brother?"
"Did you vote for George Bush?" I ask.
"I did sir," says Bob, but Brother cuts him off.

"We don't want to talk politics," says Brother,
"We want to talk about what God expects from
each and every one of us." "God has a plan."
"I had a plan too, but the tractor won't start."

"Well, we are sorry, we truly are, but we have
other folks to visit and bring God's message.
We'll just leave these magazines for you.
Now we've taken enough of your time, so . . ."

$\longrightarrow$

"Would you like some eggs?" I ask.

Brother looks back over his shoulder puzzled.

"The hens are laying good, we got lots of eggs."

"Well," says Brother, "You are kind, but we do need

to visit with others in the area and we wouldn't want

to be any bother to you when you're so busy."

"I'll just be a minute," I say and walk to the house.

I meet my wife in the cellar where we store the eggs.

"Are they gone yet?" she asks.

"I'm giving them some eggs."

"Did they ask for eggs?" she wants to know.

"If they're hungry I could make them lunch,

I just don't want to be preached at."

"Let's just give them some eggs, we got plenty."

They were both back in the Buick.

Brother rolled down the window and took the eggs.

He was blushing again. "God Bless You Sir," he says.

"Enjoy the eggs," I say. They'd left the magazines

on the tractor seat. The headline banner asked,

"What would Jesus do?" God only knows.

King Kong

Had I been a more thoughtful child in the late 1940's
when I first saw King Kong, I might have predicted
what the next sixty years would bring.
It's not the moment you're thinking of
when King Kong climbs to the top of the Empire

State Building and World War One fighter
planes unleashed hail after hail of machine
gun fire, though it's a good guess. It's not a moment
later when Kong lay dying in the street and the cop says,
"Well Denham, the airplanes got him."

And Carl Denham replies, "No, it wasn't the airplanes . . .
it was beauty that killed the beast."
Though it's a better guess and a reminder
that poetry can lie as easily as tell the truth.
No, it was when Kong was falling to his death:

the audience cheered and then for weeks after
we rode our bikes — up and down our street —
baseball cards wedged in our spokes —
a squadron of fighter planes — strafing anyone —
who lived on another street.

Echo

I am on a gurney in a darkened room having
an echocardiogram — "Just routine — just to be sure."
You know what that's like.

I listen to the whooshing, squishing, clicking and pings
while watching the blurry shapes of snow and shadow
on the monitor. I suggest to the tech that she would get

better reception with Cable.
She responds with a distracted grimace, returning
her anxious eyes to the monitor. Her face wearing

an "I can't believe what I'm seeing" squint.
Well I'm not going to stay here alone.
I leave my body on the gurney; it's all she wants,

and I go. The whooshing, squishing, clicking and pings
have put me in a watery mood. I am a humpback whale
afloat in a watery world within and without.

The echocardiogram's noises now seem a lonely song
I think I know. Or maybe it was something I heard
eons ago swimming in the endless ocean.

I think now I hear another's call
or perhaps an echo off a glacier wall?
Then all is silent, the test over.

Now she is close to me looking concerned.
"Did you fall asleep?" Her fingers find my
wrist and stealthily check my pulse.

"I didn't think you needed me, so I left."
Now she thinks I am a crazy person,
so I add, "I thought I was a whale."

Like "Moby Dick?" she says confused.
And I think of Ahab and Ishmael
and wonder if I will be the one lost at sea
or the one saved — found floating in the ocean.

Tree Swallows

It is Memorial Day weekend and a group
of old friends and neighbors have been eating,
drinking, and catching up with one another.

A brother has died. He was "never the same after
Vietnam, never had a life after, fifty years later
and the only photos he had were of army buddies."

A sister with cancer, a nephew killed in a car crash,
a family dog we all knew that had to be put down.
A horse had died in its stall and they had to get Donald

with his backhoe to pull her out to the pasture and bury her.
The mink that was killing our chickens was trapped at last.
These matters, human and country, interest us all.

Two swallows that have a nearby nest arrive
to sit on a low slung wire and rest.
She stays perched on the wire but her mate,

takes off to circle around her, to fly up behind her.
He is in the tree swallows' formal attire
and hell-bent on setting his girl on fire.

As she clings to the wire, he dips again and again
his tail flipping under hers' as hers' lifts.
It is cloacal kissing if rear ends can kiss,

and he keeps on dipping without a miss.
"What are they doing one guest asks?"
"It's birds making love," says another.

"It looks so graceful, like acrobatics or
ballet dancing on wings."
"It's sex," says another, "without the grunting."

Then it's over and as if to celebrate
they fly around the yard in lively syncopation.
"Well, that was something to see, wasn't it?"

And we all allowed how it was, wasn't it?
We are at an age when bad news far outnumbers good
And seek more than ever the solace of being understood.

So when it is time to go, we go slow, reluctant to part.
Yet that night, as we watched the guests depart,
it seemed they left with a lighter heart,
and in this, I give the swallows credit, for their part.

Cairn

Whenever I see the remains
of an old stone wall wandering
into the woods, I think of you
and our November walks.

We were supposed to be deer hunting
but if you really wanted to hunt
you'd go with Chris, who was still
young enough, to drag a deer out.

When we went hunting, it was to spend
some time together in the woods.
We would start off at our spot on a bluff
that ran along the Kinderhook,

you by the stone wall, me a hundred feet
further down the Creek, at an old maple.
The genius of the place was that across
the Creek, the corn that had grown

all summer, had now been harvested down

to stubble and scattered grain.

Deer loved the field and turkeys too,

but they were all a little too far away

to make it necessary to shoot them.

An hour of being quiet and watching

deer was about right for us.

Then you'd walk over to where I was

and we'd sit, our backs settled against thick

trees to make sure some kid out in the woods,

full of buck fever didn't shoot us.

You would tease me about buck fever

and the time I had a six point buck

in my sights. It was snowing and the buck

couldn't see me and I was so overcome

with the beauty of him coming

$\longrightarrow$

up the hill with snow on his back
I lowered my gun and shouted
for him to be careful; the woods were full
of hunters and he needed to go bed down.

You liked the story and would tell me,
"You fell in love with the buck!"
You'd seen that happen before.
Then we'd talk some about shooting
a young deer, you'd call it a "vealer"
proclaiming it the best eating deer ever.
Then you'd talk about shooting a doe
though we only ever had buck tags.

You'd say, "Why do you need antlers?"
"You can't even make soup out of them."
Only you'd call the antlers horns,
as if deer were a kind of wild cow.

Or the story of how one of your cows
got out, came crashing though our place,
then spent the summer on the mountain.
When you went up in the fall to look

for her, she saw you, walked over,

let you put a rope on her

and followed you home like a dog.

You thought she was smart;

she knew winter was coming and wanted

to spend it in a warm barn.

Others didn't believe the story, but I did.

I never saw any animal do anything

but come to you when they saw you.

We'd talk over these things and more

I can't remember. We'd come back to my

place, have a beer and a shot of scotch,

or if it was very cold a cup of coffee first.

The autumn after you died I walked

the woods alone, sat at the bluff wet-eyed,

my heart the weight of a stone.

Went deep in the woods for a walk,

then back to the old maple tree.

I waited for you to come talk,

just one last time with me.

World Enough

I have been visiting with Lottie,

the American house spider, who lives

in a dim corner of the basement.

She is always home when I visit

and I have come to rely on her company.

To be frank, I scarcely detect any greeting

on her side; so it's possible the feeling is not mutual.

Then again she holds her ground or holds her web,

and seems not to be afraid of me in the slightest.

We have an understanding. If I get my nose too close

she steps forward, lifts her front legs and *I* step back.

It is fall now and she has been here,

as long as I have lived in the house.

This can't be, since these girls only live a year,

but if it's a new girl every year,

she's the image of her mother;

long yellow legs, black bands and all.

I have been wishing lately that she could speak.

To tell me how *she* sees things. How she understands

my coming and going, and whether she wonders where I am

when I am not with her. Or if only people suffer such questions.

I think I could learn something from her.

She lives her whole life in this small triangle of space.

Imagine this small space the whole world—

and this world—world enough.

Open Mic

I am at an Open Mic evening sponsored by Inkberry
and Papyri Books. North Adams is a college town
and the assembled audience of poets and friends
were younger than I usually encounter.
Seven of us are reading and I am the eldest by so great

a margin, the younger poets could be my grandchildren.
Outer space is the most popular theme. Darth Vader appears
in one poem, light sabers and dismemberment in another.
This is not the outer space I know. My outer space
has planets and asteroids but it is mostly space,

a vast emptiness, an infinite cold, dark universe.
Their outer space is full of space ships and eccentrics.
It is a vast sea of alternate worlds where evolution
walked other paths. It is the outer space of movies and TV
populated by a script writer's imagination, special effects

and a musical score that conveniently signals whenever
something important is about to happen. Nor are their poems
anything like the poems of my youth.
Whatever became of love and all its attendant suffering?
Where is their rebelliousness?

Their heartfelt contempt for their elders?
I don't know. They're talking about outer space and they love it.
When it is my turn I read a poem about an elderly couple
gardening together for one last year before dying
and another about cows and making hay.

I look out into their young faces and they smile back
but there is a certain puzzlement too. I seem to be reminding
them of something they can't quite recall.
Later a young poet tells me that when I was reading
he kept thinking that there was a Star Trek

or maybe a Twilight Zone episode about an expedition
that finds the survivors of a much earlier group of settlers.
They were really old earthlings from another time
that to everyone's surprise were still living
in some forgotten corner of the universe.

The Speed of Light

I take a break from the wake and walk
into the dark yard behind the funeral home.
Bob, who works there, is having a cigarette.

"You need something?" he asks.
My head swivels slowly side to side.
I stand staring at a sky still full of stars.

"We see all sorts of things here,
but this one's bad," says Bob.
I don't answer. I'm beyond words.

He sighs, flips his cigarette
to the ground and walks inside.

"Anything you need," he says,
"just come to the office—anything."
I nod and turn back to the night sky.

The stars flicker with remorse.
Not only beyond words, I'm beyond feeling.
I am as cold as the dead.

I stand there a long time
and sense that somewhere,
very far away, out among the stars,
in the vastness of deep space
something has happened.

Something is coming towards us.
And it's coming at the speed of light.

Black and White

1.

I grew up in the black and white 50's
helping my mother into a Republican cloth coat
as she stopped at the hall mirror to adjust
her pill box hat and pull on her white gloves.
Well, not really.

It was a well worn Democratic coat
and kerchief and she never wore gloves.
I guess the mother I was thinking about
was from TV, only we called it "the TV"
as if it was another country with its own citizenry.

We lived in a brick and stucco house,
a two story colonial that would have been unique
except for an identical one next door.
More up to date neighbors lived in ranches.
The elite among them had that singular

status symbol of the fifties—a finished basement.
We all had linoleum floors, Formica countertops
and wall to wall carpeting. Some sophisticates
even had wall to wall on walls.
The better off had fish bowl TV's with rabbit ears,

the even better off had antennas strapped to chimneys
like crosses proclaiming America's new religion.
Before the TV, when we would watch the radio,
the living room had his and her chairs
a three-pillow couch and a low coffee table.

Next to his chair stood a magazine rack,
and a small table with a large ashtray.
Next to hers was a matching table,
and a sewing basket with the mending
and a darning egg laid neatly on top.

$\rightarrow$

Her collection of six miniature teacups
was on the mantle along with his collection
of one beer stein brought home from the war.
The room was arranged with the chairs
kitty-corner across from the couch,
as though we had conversations or even
talked to one another. When we got a TV
all seats were turned to face it
and all attempts at conversation ceased.
What blessings this new religion brought.

2.

In the black and white 50's we knew right
from wrong—wrong was what we wanted.
French postcards featuring Great Danes with
women in black bras and panties, our dreams
precipitated in black and white as compelling

as anything we had ever dreamt, though in truth
these postcard women scared us a little too.
Maybe we were not ready for them yet
but they existed, here in black and white
and so we all yearned to be photographers,

artists, and poets. People who surely knew

these women, had taken these photographs

and then we could only imagine what happened.

And imagine we did—all the time.

We were not artists yet so we had to be

content with local lusting.

Straining our eyes to see through

curtains, watching shadows on drawn shades.

Watching local nymphs in baggy blue

gym suits. Cheerleaders in short skirts

and white panties with muscular thighs

propelling them through panty flashing routines,

sent arrows of promise into our panting groins.

Dwight David Eisenhower, the last decent Republican,

was President every year I was a teenager.

He was the last black and white President.

Then there was Kennedy. Until Kennedy

it didn't seem you could go anywhere

if you started out where I did, but now

you could go the Vietnam or you could go

$\longrightarrow$

to hell, if you could tell the difference.

I was getting stoned until Kennedy's assassination

but after that grass didn't seem equal

to the weight of the times.

I moved on to LSD—the God drug.

For a while it seemed to transform my life

into everything I'd always wanted.

After a life of black and white—here was the color.

And what colors they were. The hometown I could

never escape now looked full of possibilities and man,

you could go anywhere from here. But...

why go anywhere when you were already here?

Anything gets old, even feeling like God.

I was finally getting laid by then, I married a step ahead

of the draft, had a child to stay ahead of the draft,

and then another. I worked on a career. Looking

back now I see I dipped my paddle into the water

and glided into the mainstream.

Do I have any regrets?

Doesn't everyone have regrets?

LSD became something I just didn't do anymore.

But I never forgot it and all these decades later

I still think about those years and the colors.

How I miss the color of those years.

On Doing Poetry Readings

There are moments when I am doing a poetry
reading when I look up into the listening faces,
and know our caravans have arrived together.

For they are laughing, or smiling and tearing,
or wear the stunned expression of someone
who realizes—could it be for the first time—
this is the only life any of us will ever have.

And I want to stop mid-poem to ask:
Is it something I said?
And I am amazed anew,
at what these camels can carry—
at what words can do.

The Monkey Row

I awake in the dream seated in a towering amphitheater — its
sheer stone walls strangely softened by an immense encompassing
painting of a looming ocean wave — crested and curled — foam
flying — frozen — at the brink of crashing down upon us.

The speakers stand on a small central stage, arriving
and leaving through hidden trap doors leading to underground
passageways. Seated in the inner circles closest to the speakers
are the very wealthy, an obvious aristocracy dressed in tuxedos

and gowns. The celebrity class is next, with news
anchors, movie stars, and politicians. They are followed
by circles of the military. All the Armed Forces are present,
under orders, in full dress uniform.

Next are the athletes arranged by team, from pro-teams closest
to the speakers, to college and high school teams, and finally
the children in Little League and Y summer teams. Sitting behind
so many taller athletes, the youngsters are at a disadvantage

and few can see the stage. Still there are so many of them they
almost fill the remaining seats, leaving only a few empty
rows before the monkey row. Few listen to the speakers, who
stand, one after the other, to speak — passionately gesturing like

hermit crabs. It is only the monkeys, in the uppermost row,
who are attentive, solemnly nodding their heads, each prehensile
tail holding fast to the uppermost rail. As the evening lengthens,
the monkey's rapt attention, so moves the speakers, that they

increasingly direct their remarks to the monkey row.
The people finally tire of talking among themselves,
and they too turn to watch the monkeys. The monkeys,
deep in thought, pull on their lower lips with thumb

and forefinger. They stare at the speakers with only
an occasional sidelong glance at one another.
Or at the children, a few rows below, who quietly
imitate their every gesture.

Winter Visitors

You mentioned it at
breakfast, sipping coffee
staring out the window.
We hadn't seen them at all
this winter, we missed them.

Wasn't it on a day like this
they came last winter?
Snow covering the ground
for the better part of two months.
ice crusted wherever the wind licked.

Didn't hummingbirds, you asked,
with their wrinkled pea brains
come back each spring to hover
where their feeder hung last summer?
It seemed to you a wild turkey

with a brain as big as a pecan
could remember where they found
food in winter. The crabapples
were full of turkeys last winter,
so many heavy birds they bent

and even broke branches. Now too
the crabapples are covered with fruit,
even the old apple tree has frozen fruit
clinging to limbs beyond ladder's reach.
Two hours later I call you to the window.

A large flock of turkeys had come
from the woods crossing the east field
in a ragged single line, breaking
through the crust ice every few steps.
A column of refugees, limping and exhausted

trying to out walk death.
They went to the weedy edges bordering
the field and worked their way round
drifting in and out of the woody margins,
pecking dispiritedly at weed heads.

Then they saw the crabapples. In an instant
two dozen joyful wild turkeys, their feathers
flashing black and tan, the color of wet bark
and bright copper, were feeding in the trees
and on the fruit falling to the snow below.   →

They clustered there a long while
then moved off single file to a stand
of hemlocks beyond the stream.
Winter visitors enjoying the gift
of summer fruit in February…

summoned do you think by your
thoughts? Or was it their coming
that turned your thoughts to them?
They leave in their wake more evidence,
because more is always needed,

of what we do not know.
Of how much passes unaware
between us all.
Of this much we can be sure—
there is more…there is more.

No!

She ran after the ball as the car . . .

No!

She saw the car just in time . . .

No!

The driver saw her just in time . . .

No!

The car hit her . . .

The driver rushed us to the hospital . . .

She was checked and released . . .

No!

The car hit her . . . she is screaming . . .

We are in an ambulance . . . siren blaring

The EMT's are scared . . . I am shivering with fear . . .

But . . . we make it . . . after many weeks . . . she comes home . . .

No!

The car hit her . . .

No!

No!

No!

Hurray for Hollywood

We have been watching the banditos
slowly make their way up the mountain.
We were hoping they hadn't seen us
but by now it is clear they have.

We are behind large boulders
and their leader, a grizzled man
in a gold hat calls up to us saying
they are the Federales.

Dobbs wants to see their badges.
"Badges? We ain't got no badges.
We don't need no badges.
I don't have to show you any stinkin badges."

Then we all start shooting.
This is when the real Federales
show up and run the bandits off.
I never liked Dobbs; he was no one to mess

with and later, after he shot Curtain,
I was happy the bandits killed him.
This was the sort of life and justice
I found only at the movies.

I was just off camera in that scene,
in the rocks above Dobbs.
Actually, I guess, way off camera.
I was nine years old and seated

in a movie theater in Hicksville, Long Island.
But I remember that gunfight better than
anything else that happened that year.
And the scene in "Stardust Memory" when

Sandy Bates is looking at Dorrie, the moment
he says is the happiest in his life.
Oh God, I loved that crazy woman, we both did.
She is lying on the floor and the music slowly

gets louder and it's Louie Armstrong playing "Stardust",
the time he adds "Oh Memory, Oh Memory, Oh Memory"
to the lyrics and Dorrie looks up at Sandy and me and smiles.
A smile of such warmth, sweetness and sultry promise,

it's not just Sandy's happiest memory; it's mine too.
At the movies I find a life equal to who I really am,
not the person you know, but the real one, the one
I become when the lights are lowered.

Big Joe

It is the night of Big Joe's Polka Party in Valentine, Nebraska. The old Grange Hall is full of friends and neighbors enjoying a night out. The steam tables are set up along the right wall and the beer and cash bar is set up on . . . the other right wall. Which wall is the right wall depends on whether you prefer beer or kielbasa or whether you came in the front door or the back door. Either way, the food and the beer are brought to you courtesy of the Valentine Volunteer Fire Department.

The band has arrived and sets up as we finish our meals.

Looking around at my neighbors you'd think we must have lined up, the 6 and ½ footers down to the 4 and ½ footers, the 280 pounders down to the 90 pounders, and been paired up in a Nebraska Aggie cross-pollination trial. As a result each member of every couple is as different from their partner as the senior citizen gene pool of Cherry County will allow. But, despite appearances, it didn't happen that way. It happened the usual way, kids meeting in high school or at work though around here most of us grew up always knowing each other.

We're easy to make fun of. We do it ourselves all the time but, just as you might start to laugh, Frankie Yablonski calls out to his band– 1-2-3-4-2-3-4 and the music begins to swirl around the room like a dust devil and gets the couples up. We push our chairs back and walk slowly to the dance floor. We reach out to lay hold on each other and in a moment, like the day winter becomes spring, we are transformed. We are liquid now and we are dancing. Dancing better than a lot of us can walk, the way a boy with a stutter can sing better than he can talk.

We dance seriously, purposefully, like we do everything. Like Warren here dancing next to us landed on Omaha Beach and after the war got up every morning at six, six days a week to be at the hardware store by seven. Like his wife Mary nursed their boy Silas day and night for a week until he finally beat the pneumonia. The way, that for her, it was nothing special, just something that needed doing. It's the way we are. Whether it's landing on Omaha Beach, weeding the garden or carrying over a meal for a sick neighbor. When things need doing, we try to get them done.

$\rightarrow$

None of us is much for talking. Whatever needed saying has been said by now or never will be. Talk can only carry a person so far. To go further you need music and with the band well into the Hot Foot polka or maybe it's the Red Barn polka, we have the music the way we like it. We know why we came out this March night. It's for the music, the way it moves through you, knocking the mud off your feet and troubles out of your head. Now they are doing "In Heaven there is No Beer" and we are singing along, "In Heaven there is no beer, that's why we have to drink it here."

Oh, we are going to ache in the morning, but it doesn't matter. We have a plan. After breakfast we'll clear the dishes and sit side by side at the kitchen table. We will look through the seed catalogs that have been coming one or two a week since January. We practically have them memorized by now and it's time to get the seed order in.

It is coming onto spring in Nebraska and we're not done with living yet.

Proof

I was thinking of writing a poem
proving the existence of God.

Your smile is item number one . . .
though I couldn't help but notice
you could use a little orthodontia.

Your heavenly body is item number two . . .
though, it could also use some work,
a tuck here or there, a little lipo, a bit of botox.

I hate to be superficial,
but it's the surface we see.
Whatever may lie below,

say the cutest kidney in the city,
might be a source of inner delight,
but it's hard to see, even in good light.

Is there proof God exists?

The debate has raged for ages,
while the proof of orthodontist's
can be found in the Yellow Pages.

On Reading Poe Late at Night

Of course I turn to you when I feel the pull
of Morpheus's emissary. Is not sleep but
next of kin to living in the ossuary?

Why do we need to rehearse the final scene?
Where is the art in lying in the ground?

Of course I turn to rouse you round,
though stealthily without a sound.
Oh, let us not sleep, but take flight
from the night in libidinal delight.

I negotiate the nightgown's flannel fortress.
Stealthily I connive a path past alligator
zippers and clasps of wire. Oh, why
must you come to bed dressed like a friar?

"I'm sleeping," you groan, "leave me alone."

"You're not sleeping, you're talking to me."

"Please shut up! I have to go to work in the morning."

"Alright," I say, "fair is fair" and relenting,
return my thoughts to Poe in whispered recitation:

"Once upon a midnight dreary as I pondered weak and weary
there came a tapping at my chamber door. Eagerly I wished
the morrow, had sought surcease of sorrow—sorrow
for the lost Lenore."

"Who's Lenore?" she says.

"I think it's Poe's girlfriend, she's dead."
You know, "Quoth the Raven 'Nevermore'."

"Oh … why can't you be normal?" she says.

"Why don't you go sleep with Lenore?"

Me and Lucille

I was at the Rite Aid last night
killing time . . .
waiting for it to kill me . . . and still
searching for the fountain of youth.

I was reading the directions
on a promising potion
when I looked up and saw Lucille.
My heart leaped, tripped, toppled and fell.

It took a long moment to remember
Lucille would be seventy-four in November
and this girl looked seventeen.
Lucille was the first girl I dated

in my wet dreams. The girl who inspired
me to write poetry and ruined my life.
I was thirteen when the "Siren of Sycamore"
was seventeen and I was invisible.

But I've written enough about Lucille,
too many Lucille's. This poem's about me.
Red-faced, zit-sprinkled, clumsy me.
I did almost run into her on my Schwinn

once. Peddling along silently following
her behind when she half turned
in that woman of the world, Ingrid
Bergman way and I forgot how to steer.

She shouted "stupid" as I bounced off the curb
into traffic. That was the only time she spoke
to me except for the time she ruined my life.
The year I turned thirteen I spent

my birthday money on a pocket
knife. A stainless steel folder with
horn handles and a genuine leather sheath.
I kept it secret for weeks practicing,

mastering, the celebrated toe-knee-chest-nut
of knife tricks. At last I was ready
for the front yard or the circus and here,
what could be better, was Lucille walking by

and actually stopping as some younger
boys watched the show.
Toe . . . knee . . . chest . . . worked
perfectly with the knife flipping

$\rightarrow$

end over end and diving into the grass.
Now for the pinnacle of skill, the drop
from the nut. I took a deep breath,
looked at Lucille the way Clark Gable

looked at Vivian Leigh in "Gone with the Wind"
and let the knife drop. The boys gasped
and stepped back. Lucille spoke her first complete
sentence to me. "The knife is sticking in your foot."

"I did it on purpose," I said.
Then Lucille spoke her last complete sentence to me.
"You're even stupider than I thought you were."
I'm there now. My fountain of youth

leaking warm blood into my shoe,
the color rising on my face.
Staring at Lucille's behind
as she slowly walks down Sycamore.

March 21st

It's too early to do any gardening now,
the shady corner holds crusty snow.
Stones, frost heaved from deep below,
prehistoric teeth that grimace in a row
shows the first harvest — one we didn't sow.

I'm walking my land, though mine, by only
the thinnest convention. I'm hardly the only
owner here. Owners with rightful claims are
endless. Foremost, is the land itself, without it,
I would be no place.

I've lived here twenty years but many others
in this congregation are on their thousandth generation.
Some so small they can't be seen at all.
Some like bears as big as me, some we always see,
others we know only from track or spore,

howling or rustling in the night setting our hackles upright.
Winter's done. Some have lived, some died.
We know some of the how; none of the why.
Walking around, looking around, so much asks to be understood.
It's clearly coming into spring now and — don't that sun feel good?

Folksinger at the Senior Center

A poem for Marilyn Miller

Marilyn smiles the moment she lifts
the guitar into her embrace. Another
moment of arched eyebrow concentration
to tickle her baby into tune, and she begins.

She's playing a song she's written about a young
girl who wants to go dancing, and a mother who
blames her own unhappiness on her love of dancing
and musicians. The girl wants to go — the mother

pleads with her — to not repeat her mistakes.
As if it were part of the performance,
some high school girls, volunteers here, have started
dancing. Marilyn's smile broadens. The girls move

in a limber smoothness — powered by high-octane hormones —
that are a fond memory for most of us in the audience.
To watch them, as we are all doing now, is to remember
how our stiff bodies once responded to music, how

each note would play us and move through us.
Even now the power of music cannot be denied.
Whatever was on my mind when I arrived
has been blown away in the sounds freshening breeze.

Another chorus and I am smiling too, tapping a stiff foot
and singing along. My foot has gotten happy
and the happy rises through me in a joyous rush.
This is why I am here, for the music,

to experience it live, for the young dancers, for
the way it flows and swells, lifting even my leaden soul
into the notes, the lyrics and the story.
The song swells into a twanging cascading flood of sound.

We are all singing now and I am carried into the moment
I have been longing for — when all there is — is song.
The moment I want to live in. Light as air — lifted in song.
The story of the struggle, of mother and daughter,

the gravity of experience against the buoyancy of youth.
Oh how persuaded I am against my own aged judgment.
The song ends, and the applause, like a wave, tosses me
onto dry land. And I have to pee.

Product Placement – Making Big Bucks in Poetry

I shut off my Sony 32" HD TV and went to get ready. I carried my Starbuck's coffee in with me, placing it on the Ikea nightstand. I showered with Head and Shoulders shampoo and washed with fresh smelling Irish Spring soap. I dried myself with a luxurious Cannon bath towel from Bed, Bath and Beyond.

Grandma was dead. I dressed quickly in my Kenneth Cole Suit from Men's Wearhouse that goes so well with my blue Arrow shirt and patterned Bugatchi tie. I drove my Honda Accord to the (this space still available) Funeral Home.

My sexy cousin Marsha arrived the same time I did. She looked fetching in her Anne Klein dress and Andiamo high heels. She had flown in on American Airlines and was staying at the Marriott. We hugged and she whispered her room number in my ear. The service was just beginning as we entered the Chapel. Grandma had been old, and sadly hadn't been able to remember me last time I visited, though thanks to Aricept her decline had been very gradual. In fact, Grandma hadn't been able to remember herself the last time I saw her, though she could still sing all the stanzas to "See the USA in your Chevrolet."

The service was very touching and Marsha and I grew teary. I handed her my Kleenex pocket pack. She held my hand and played with my Timex Indiglo, flashing it on and off like a firefly in heat while I got high on her Chanel #5. I was glad I remembered to take my Cialis. I think the Nature's Way ginkgo biloba is really working.

Photo Album

Why do I faithfully carry my dead parent's
photo album, like ashes, from home to home?
Eighteen pages of coarse black paper bound
by shoelaces between faux leather covers.

Eight tiny black and white photos on a page,
each placed in black corner tabs that lack
the strength to hold this world in place.
None of the photos is labeled.

Who would have imagined these people,
these events could ever be forgotten.
Yet I turn the pages unable to attach names
to these vaguely familiar faces. I remember

only the photographs. Is this a memory
or the remains of a memory?
Even when I find myself in a photo
at four or five, looking up at me across

so many years, surrounded

by Tanta's and Bubba's, we seem

only another group of wandering Jews —

émigrés from one lost world – lost in another.

New Religion

I've been working on this new religion.
No commandments — too heavy-handed — we're going
with affirmations or perhaps pointers for the pious.

Some aspects of the new religion will sound familiar;
the basic essentials. Keep your hands off your neighbor's ass,
try not to steal, try harder not to murder.

We go to heaven — they don't. The marketing guys think
an incentive is important. Beyond the basics, I've picked
the best of the best from other religions.

A small example; our pious women will wear burqas
with high heels and nothing underneath.
A fine point but important to some.

And certain things are too traditional to change.
So we encourage the chosen people to treat the earth
like we won it in a card game.

Promise the people a great life in heaven if we can screw
them on earth. Uncle Bernie thought it sounded
like every other religion though he admitted

the part about the burqas and the high heels

might sway him to convert, as long as

we don't tell my Aunt.

Now I haven't told anyone this next part except for Cousin Julius.

I'm the Supreme Leader and live forever.

Julius said, forget about it; the science doesn't work,

then Julius said if I wanted to do this I should

have done it in the desert a thousand years ago.

He has a point, starting a new religion today is expensive,

all the TV spots, the operators . . . I mean . . . the prayer partners

standing by. Julius said, no one's going to believe in a new religion,

But I've studied religion, finding believers' is easy.

What's hard is not getting killed by people from another religion.

Then I got creative. We could offer life insurance to converts,

martial arts classes and protective religious charms at 20% off.

The Rabbi's Annoyed

The Rabbi's annoyed. The latest Reform prayer book
makes scant mention of Olam Ha-Ba; the world to come.

"Why does that bother you?" I ask,
"You don't believe in heaven or hell."

"Listen my enlightened friend; visit hospice with me,
 then you will understand the dying need heaven."

"You tell them they're going to heaven?"

"I tell them they are going on a journey we all must take,
I tell them as one door closes, another opens."

"Do you tell them the ones who went before are waiting?"

"Not waiting," says the Rabbi, "waiting with outstretched arms.
They're dying; would you deny them pain medicine?
Would you look into their eyes and say, this is it?

"Here comes nothing, and it's nothing forever.
Imagine meeting your first forever ever
and it's the last forever you'd ever want?

"You think reality is wonderful?
You think people have run from reality
for thousands of years because it's wonderful?"

"Doesn't reality matter?" I ask.

"Listen my rational, healthy friend, the final day will come
for you and for me. And on that day if a kind soul tells you
the coffin's lid is Heaven's Gate — you won't want to debate.

Nuns in Motion

There's a law in Newtonian physics about inertia,

which states things at rest tend to remain at rest,

while things in motion tend to remain in motion.

But Isaac Newton didn't know nuns.

Nuns could be dozing at their desk one minute and running

toward you, at the speed of light swinging a ruler, the next.

Or so it seemed to me, a lucky public school student,

who heard accounts of nuns from friends in Catholic School.

I admit I always watched nuns—nuns being something

of an obsession for Jewish kids. I watched them, with a mixture

of awe and fear, the kind of feelings most kids had about Army

veterans. The ones with missing legs who swung down Main Street

on crutches with pant legs, neatly pressed, folded and safety pinned.

Unlike veterans, who were always alone, nuns walked around town

in groups of three or four in black habits; their faces girdled by

stiff white wimples. The young ones would smile, the older

ones had lost the capacity, but would occasionally nod gravely.
Then, overnight, the wimples were gone, the habits shortened,
and nuns were wearing flowers in their hair and playing guitars.
A few years later and you couldn't find a nun under eighty.

It was a nun who told my friend Matt the problem
with Christianity is that it's never been tried,
which is the same thing my father said about Communism.
When I told my father what the nun told Matt,

he said he didn't think the nun would last long.
When Matt told a priest what the nun said, and then
because he felt bad, added what my father said
about Communism, the priest thought they both had it right,

and if Christianity and Communism were tried,
they'd be hard to tell apart. I told that to my father
and he didn't think the priest
was going to last very long either.

Kindling

I'm gathering kindling on a late November day.
Work the hands do on their own, freeing
my thoughts to float with the apparent
aimlessly of silently falling flakes of snow.

The small branches I'm collecting have lain
on the forest floor since last winter and snap
with the resonant crack of seasoned kindling.
Not green wood that bends round, nor rotting

sticks more mold than meat. The ones I want are dry,
ready for their final flash, to fire the heavy quarter-
rounds for heat then ash for the spring garden.
For company I have a few chickadees who inspect

each leaf I disturb, half a dozen juncos,
who appear with the first snow, and small clusters
of crows standing in the clearing like pallbearers.
Yesterday was a friend's funeral. A man I knew

long and well. A difficult fellow, a poor choice
for a friend though in truth no worse than me.
It's colder today in these woods than it was yesterday.
Yet I am warm now and yesterday I would have sworn

we were witness to a new ice age. And the weather
wasn't the only strangeness. There was another.
His brother was there, an ordinary matter, except
he looks so much like my friend, it was as though

he was attending his own funeral, like an actor playing
two roles in the same movie. A movie with a surprise
ending. Not for any of us standing graveside,
but for my friend who thought the cancer

would pass the way other things had. He never
did admit how sick he was. In time we gave up trying
to talk with him about it. What's the point?
It's not easy to die and who knows

$\longrightarrow$

if there's a right way to do it?
These little birds might, the crows must,
but it's not a thing they'd share with us.
Still, I felt not being able to talk with him about dying

was a pity though I'm not exactly sure whose pity.
I find myself thinking, now that he's dead,
what am I supposed to do? Stand around till I'm dead?
Till everyone I know is dead? I know some would say,
Why do anything? Or, there's nothing to be done.
But, of course, a man needs to do something —
that's a difference between men and women —
woman can sit with things, a man needs to do.

So I am collecting kindling. Thinking it's good
to do a needful thing with the cold coming on.

American Exports

For Dan Wilcox

They don't like us watching when the kids come back
on gurneys, in caskets. American exports,
stamped "Return to Sender."

Kids playing soldiers, who give so much, ask for so little,
and never get it from the people who send them, who give
so little, take so much, and never get what they deserve.

While the rest of us — live large — working two jobs
or no jobs, watching American Idol, getting Foxed — Fair
and Balanced — munching wings, getting foreclosed.

War — America's number one export. Nothing we'd want here,
but hey, we're saving the world, been at it for decades,
shock and awe — America's business. And if you think

war is bad or our music is destroying your youth —
wait till McDonalds and Kentucky Fried Chicken get there.
In a couple of years you'll be begging for mercy . . . and insulin.

Robert Frost's Soft-boiled Egg

In the nineteen fifties Robert Frost occasionally did readings in New York City. When he did his friend and printer, Joseph Blumenthal of Spiral Press and his wife Ann, would host a reception for him after the reading. The reception would be at the Blumenthal apartment. When Mr. Frost arrived at the apartment, his hostess Ann Blumenthal would take him to the kitchen and make him a soft-boiled egg. They would sit together for 20 minutes as he ate the egg and then Mr. Frost, feeling restored would join the guests. (Reported by Jack Hagstrom, MD, a friend of Frost, in a talk at The Stone House Museum, September 19, 2010)

Ann knew Frost well enough
to see the lonely child.
Frost knew Ann well enough
to trust she saw the child.

They understood the worth
of a soft-boiled egg, the worth
of a warm, quiet kitchen —
a knowing recognition —
healing home remedies
amid adult activities.

Ann's presence soothed Frost
And the egg restored him.

Or the egg soothed Frost
And Ann's presence restored him.

It wouldn't have worked without Ann.
It wouldn't have worked without an egg.

Uncle Jess

I woke this morning thinking of you,
a surprise until I remembered
it's the anniversary of your death,
your thirtieth Yahrzeit.

We are at an age when Yahrzeit
candles stand like wax memories
waiting to be lit into davening flames.
 I decide to light one for you and me.

You never believed in God or the religion
you were born to — your religion was revolution.
My mother thought your union organizing,
with its countless hours of work, traveling

endlessly from one factory or mine to another,
was a sad mistake that robbed you of a family
of your own and a home which was her idea
of a normal life.

You thought my mother was a good cook,

but hopelessly bourgeois. How odd

to think of that word now. I can't remember

the last time I heard anyone accused of being

bourgeois, now that everyone is.

Your stories about strikes and scabs, industrialists

and workers, greed and injustice, made you a hero

to me. This troubled my mother who would say

after your visits. "Poor Uncle Jess is as skinny

as a stray cat and as poor as one because

he never took time to have a family or a real job . . .

always the dreamer . . ." She'd mutter shaking her head.

Those last years, when you were slowed by illness,

you turned to your beloved abstract painting.

You had mellowed a little and, for the first time,

had time to spend with me. I was in graduate school

→

by then and brought bagels to your tiny apartment.
You'd make tea and we'd eat and discuss
economics and history, your life as an organizer
and always the revolution.

Uncle Jess, I am sorry to tell you, the poor are poorer,
the rich are richer and the people are still
being duped into voting against themselves.
Russia is now run, not by Communists,
but by robber barons who are first cousins
to the thugs you fought for so many years.
The revolution looks further away than ever.
You would've had a laugh over my telling

you these things as though you could hear me.
But I know I'm talking to myself. Still, I like
remembering you. Something you would have known
is the only Yahrzeit that really matters.

Honeybee

A honeybee lands on the back of my hand,
licks the salty damp with the patient persistence
of a cat; her tongue, a pink straw edged in black.

She hovers gently from gleam to glisten
stirring breezes that whisper of dandelion suns,
yellow beacons glowing in the green and sultry
currents of sweet lilac flowing in the spring air.

She fills her crop with my gift of perspiration,
gossips of drones' missions of ecstasy and death,
the sweet companionship of a thousand sisters,
the devotion of all to their mother — the queen.

This fray-winged worker who will not last the season
has touched me in a way that lies beyond all reason.

Ours is a lonely world and relations are never certain,
yet this bee allowed a glimpse through nature's curtain,
and demonstrates, though indifferent to our final fate,
nature will offer gifts — if we are still and wait.

Rain

I fall asleep to the sound of rain falling.
We are in the rundown hill town upstate,
or the ramshackle B&B in Gloucester.
The place it rained for days and smelled
like coffee in the morning then boiled
cabbage all afternoon.

Was it there we set the record?

Our Guinness for the most days rejoicing in bed?

Or was it at the tiny board and batten cabin on the lake
the summer between college and graduate school.
Remember the ghost of the lake rising each evening to haunt
the pine woods? How the sun rising over the eastern hills
and the plop, plop, plop of fish teased us awake?

Was it the summer we refused to have a clock? The summer
of meditation, of living in the moment? The whole summer,
one long August afternoon of reading each other by braille,
grasping and barely grasping what we had in hand.

Listening to the music you called —
"our song" — the crickets playing strings,
the birds on flute . . . the cicada's electric solo.

That's how I remember it in my dreams.
You were the girl I loved my senior year in high school,
the one I was afraid to ask out, the one who went away
to college and disappeared from my waking life.

What could I do but disappear from waking life myself?

Passing the light of day distracting myself
from the loneliness and longing,
until the night, because . . .
you come with the night
to the sound of falling rain,
slipping into my dream
as though this was the life
you too had chosen.

The Moon and the Giant Impactor Theory

The theory is that about four and a half billion years ago, the Earth, only fifty million years old, experienced the largest impact event in its history. This giant collision vaporized the upper layers of Earth's mantle, and ejected large amounts of debris into Earth orbit. Our Moon formed from this debris. (Wikipedia, "Giant Impact Hypothesis")

Writing about the moon is fine once in a blue moon,
but if I keep writing more poems about the moon
people will think I'm a lunatic. I can't help myself.

I keep thinking about that stunned stone-face
clotting together out of the shared stroke of expulsion.
Like a puppy abandoned at the side of the road

who follows the disappearing car — so the moon
follows the earth — so I follow you.
Maybe the moon is the sum of all that has been

forsaken — certainty, trust, belief, place — maybe that's
why we trouble the moon with our longing,
succumb to its sadness, echo its madness monthly.

I keep returning to the moon as a metaphor,

hoping if I can get it right, I can finally mourn

for the earth and the moon, though I will never

stop mourning for what we were, once upon a time

when we were one. As earth and moon dance

on alone, we too must orbit on our own.

Forever together . . . forever apart

tethered by the gravity of a broken heart.

This Here Guy

When I was a kid we had a neighbor, a retired guy,
I would visit and help with chores.
Frank was the only grown-up I ever called by his first name;
unless my parents were around, then I called him Mr. M
because no one could pronounce his last name.
He had a workshop in his garage, a pigeon loft full
of Flying Flights, and a garden that was more tomatoes
than anything else. All summer long he'd send me to one
neighbor or another with gifts of tomatoes "from Mr. M."
If he was outside, he was most days during summer vacation,
he was glad for my company. In the early mornings,
then again in the late afternoons, if it wasn't too hot,
we'd chase up his Flights and try to catch some strays.

I was only in the third or fourth grade, but even then,
I knew the way he talked wouldn't last a minute in school,
which was a shame because I liked it better
than the regular boring English everybody else spoke.
What was special about him, aside from liking me,
was the way he talked. He never said,
"Hand me the hammer," It was always,
"This here hammer," unless he meant the other one,
and then he'd say, "That there hammer."

This grammar applied to everything; once when I met

his grown up daughter, he introduced me by saying,

"This here boy lives next door and helps me

with this here garden." Then introduced her by saying,

"This here's my youngest, Mary. She lives down there in the city."

She didn't talk like Frank.

In the pigeon loft he'd say, "Now see this here bird?

It's from that there pair, and that there bird,"

pointing for clarity's sake, "is from this here pair."

He used "now" a lot too, "Now you see this here tomato,

it's from seed I got from my father."

It wasn't the now of now as opposed to earlier or later,

it was a now that wasn't in the dictionary; I know, I looked.

I looked again when I wrote this, and it's in the better dictionary

I use now, but it's way down as number eight in the definitions.

Anyway the thing is, I liked that there guy Frank,

and though he died when I was eleven or twelve,

I still think of him as the first person to start me thinking

about words. What I'm saying in this here poem is;

"Thanks, Frank!" What I'm telling you is;

more than any English teacher, that there guy,

got this here guy, interested in poetry.

About God

Even when I don't believe in God I believe there is something
not to believe in. I think this is hard-wired in us for the moments
when our despair outweighs any possible hope, and we could
not go on if we had to go on alone.

For those times, God, like an invisible silverback gorilla,
who can provide the most improbable reversals of fortune,
for the price of a prayer—at those times—
the existence of God is certain.

Even when things are going well and I'm grateful, it is helpful
to have God to focus on, like a gently swinging watch hanging
from the hypnotist's pale hand.

Still, I have my problems with God. Take 9/11 for example,
not the worst thing that ever happened, unless it happened to you.
I keep wondering what if all the hijackers had woken up
with the flu that morning, and between throwing up and running
to the toilet, were too sick to be terrorists?

How hard would that have been for a God who does
that sort of thing to a few thousand people every day?
It makes you wonder if God is our silverback or theirs.
Or if God is impartial letting us do what we want,
the way two kids fight it out in a schoolyard without the teacher
stopping them. Why doesn't the teacher stop them?

Or maybe there are many Gods like the ancients said and we
have a God and they have a God and maybe there are more—
a God for people who are sick and a God for people
who are well; a God for the natives and a God for the colonials;
a God for the people who died in Hiroshima
and a God for the crew of the Enola Gay.

Maybe there is a God for believers and a God for atheists;
a God for lovers and another for those who never find love.
Maybe we all have our own personal God
and there are as many Gods as there are of us and they
don't know what they're doing anymore than we do.

For myself I can't figure out if God is on our side, not on our side,
doesn't take sides, doesn't care, or just doesn't exist.

So I was thinking that maybe we should stop talking to God
and start talking to each other, which—for all we know—
is all we have.

Paradise

I've been thinking about time.
It's picking up speed since
the grave's gravity increases
as its distance decreases.

Behind me the past retreats
into a slide show, a handful of moments
standing clear; here I'm eight;
there thirteen, nothing happened in between.

The present fades. This is no Sunday
drive ending where it began. It would
be good to have a goal but Paradise is further
away than it appears in the rearview mirror.

You don't have to be a blind man to see
Paradise is what we've lost.
Not what we've escaped or survived;
that was only childhood.

Let it go. It's not where we're going.
Keep writing poems of wonder and dread.
Don't try to leave the world a better place,
we've done enough damage.

No more utopias, no more heavens on earth.
Let's not follow our erection in that direction;
the earth can't take anymore.
Relax, no need to ask for directions;

it's not something we'd do anyway.
Let's let ourselves be carried,
we're on our way — can you feel it?
As we slow down, we're gaining speed.

About the Poet

Howard J. Kogan is a social worker/psychotherapist who lives with his wife Libby in the Taconic Mountains of New York State where he enjoys the rural life and writing. About his writing he says, "after setting aside writing poetry in my twenties to attend to family and career, I returned to it in my sixties. I am grateful to have this opportunity to return to an early love. I think of it as my Indian summer, a season of sun and tranquility nestled between the foreshadowing of what is to come and its final arrival."

Award-Winning Poems from the
Smith's Tavern Poet Laureate Contest
compiled by Sunday Four Poets

Each year in April the poets of New York's Capital Region make their annual pilgrimage to Voorheesville, a quiet upstate village nestled among the shadows of the Helderberg Escarpment in western Albany County. They are inspired by the quest to have their name engraved upon "the Willie," the coveted trophy given to the poet crowned as Laureate of Smith's Tavern. The contest, a rousing success since its inception, is organized by the Sunday Four Poets, an open-mic poetry forum dedicated to continuing the rich cultural legacy of Voorheesville and the adjacent hilltowns.

2010 Edition
$9.95

2011 Edition
Available October 2011

ORDER ONLINE AT WWW.SQUARECIRCLEPRESS.COM

CPSIA information can be obtained at www.ICGtesting.com
Printed in the USA
243205LV00004B/2/P